THE SANDY LAKE TRAGEDY

Following in the Footsteps of the Ojibwe

by
Emily Faith Johnson

content consulting by
Nicholas Bimibatoo Mishtadim DeShaw
Outreach Coordinator, American Indian Studies, University of Minnesota

CAPSTONE PRESS
a capstone imprint

Published by Capstone Press, an imprint of Capstone
1710 Roe Crest Drive, North Mankato, Minnesota 56003
capstonepub.com

Copyright © 2026 by Capstone. All rights reserved. No part of this publication may be reproduced in whole or in part, or stored in a retrieval system, or transmitted in any form or by any means, electronic, mechanical, photocopying, recording, or otherwise, without written permission of the publisher.

Library of Congress Cataloging-in-Publication Data is available on the Library of Congress website.

ISBN: 9798875206139 (hardcover)
ISBN: 9798875206146 (paperback)
ISBN: 9798875206153 (ebook PDF)

Summary: In 1850, 5,000 Ojibwe people were forced to make a dangerous journey across the Midwest to get treaty payments owed to them from the U.S. government. But the payments never came, and the Ojibwe had to travel back home through treacherous winter conditions and without the money or supplies they had been promised. More than 400 Ojibwe lost their lives in this event that is now known as the Ojibwe Trail of Tears. Discover more about the injustices of this forced removal, the many consequences, and why this tragedy is still vitally relevant today.

Editorial Credits
Designer: Jaime Willems; Media Researcher: Svetlana Zhurkin; Production Specialist: Katy LaVigne

Image Credits
Alamy: Science History Images, 4, 17; Associated Press: John Locher, 29; Bridgeman Images: Peter Newark American Pictures, 13, Photo © North Wind Pictures, 14; Capstone: Jaime Willems (beadwork design elements), cover and throughout; Getty Images: enjoynz (texture), cover and throughout, Hulton Archive, 11, Jonathan Kozub/NHLI, 5, mikroman6, 7, PeterHermesFurian, 21 (base map); Library of Congress: 15, 25; National Archives and Records Administration: General Records of the United States Government, 9; The New York Public Library: The Miriam and Ira D. Wallach Division of Art/Prints and Photographs/Photography Collection, cover (top), 1, 12; Science Source: ArcticPhoto/B & C Alexander, 18; Shutterstock: Dan Thornberg, cover (bottom), Linda McKusick, 19, melissamn, 16, Richard A. McGuirk, 20; Smithsonian Institution: National Portrait Gallery/gift of Barry Bingham, Sr., 10; SuperStock: Artokoloro, 23 (top), Newberry Library/Artist–Seth Eastman, 6; U.S. Army Corps of Engineers: Patrick Loch, 28; Wisconsin Historical Society: 8 (#WHI-42457), 23 (middle, # WHI-3957), 24 (#TP175035), 26 (#WHI-3351), 27 (#WHI-109506)

The full version of the top photo on the cover can be seen on page 12, which shows a group of Ojibwe men and a dog, taken in Duluth, Minnesota, around 1843.

Beadwork design elements are inspired by authentic Ojibwe beaded artifacts from the mid- to late 19th century.

Any additional websites and resources referenced in this book are not maintained, authorized, or sponsored by Capstone. All product and company names are trademarks™ or registered® trademarks of their respective holders.

Direct quotations appear on the following pages:

Page 10, "…[we] feel ourselves aggrieved…" and page 22, "When we left for home…" from a letter to Luke Lea, Commissioner of Indian Affairs, Washington, D.C., written by Chief Gichi-Weshki (Buffalo) and other tribal leaders, November 6, 1851, chequamegonhistory.com/tag/chief-buffalo-of-la-pointe/
Accessed November 18, 2024.

Pages 14 and 17, "…the portion for an adult…" from a quote by Chief Bagone-giizhig (Hole-in-the-Day the Younger) at a public hearing in St. Paul, Minnesota, undated, mnopedia.org/event/sandy-lake-tragedy
Accessed November 18, 2024.

Pages 18 and 20, "Tell him I blame him…" from a message by Chief Eshkibagikoonzhe (Flat Mouth) to Alexander Ramsey about John Watrous, December 3, 1850, hmdb.org/m.asp?m=206878
Accessed November 18, 2024.

Printed and bound in China. 6274

TABLE OF CONTENTS

Introduction 4

CHAPTER 1
Life in the Great Lakes 6

CHAPTER 2
A Devious Scheme 10

CHAPTER 3
Broken Promises 14

CHAPTER 4
The Long March 18

CHAPTER 5
A Chief and a President 22

Remembering Sandy Lake 28
Timeline of Sandy Lake Events 30
Glossary 31
Read More 31
Internet Sites 31
About the Author 32
Index 32

INTRODUCTION

The Ojibwe are one of the largest Indigenous groups in North America. They have lived in the areas surrounding the Great Lakes in both the United States and Canada for centuries. In 1850–1851, the U.S. government was responsible for the forced removal of the Ojibwe people, causing more than 400 deaths. This is the story of how the Ojibwe persevered and won the fight to stay on their land.

Fact
The Ojibwe are also known as the Ojibway, Ojibwa, Chippewa, or Anishinaabe.

Traditional Ojibwe village in Michigan, 1840s

Young Anishinaabe girls sing before a hockey game in Canada.

ABOUT THE OJIBWE

- In the 1850s, there were about 9,000 Ojibwe people in the United States. Today there are about 250,000 Ojibwe in the U.S.

- There are 21 federally recognized Ojibwe tribes, most in the Great Lakes region.

- The traditional Ojibwe language is called Anishinaabemowin.

- Historically the Ojibwe were known for trading, intricate beadwork, use of birchbark, and harvesting wild rice.

- From the late 1700s to the mid-1800s, the U.S. government signed dozens of treaties with the Ojibwe, forcing them to give up more and more of their land.

- The Ojibwe follow the Seven Grandfather Teachings: wisdom, love, respect, bravery, honesty, humility, and truth.

CHAPTER 1
LIFE IN THE GREAT LAKES

"The land where food grows on water" —from an Ojibwe prophecy

According to Ojibwe oral history, the ancestors of the Ojibwe nation once lived near the Atlantic Ocean, but an ancient prophecy told them to travel west to find "the land where food grows on water." When they arrived at the Great Lakes, they discovered the wild rice growing there and realized this was the food they were supposed to find. The wild rice soon became one of the main food sources for the Ojibwe. The area also had abundant fish and wild game, and vast forests of maple trees for collecting sweet sap.

Ojibwe women gathering wild rice

FACT
As well as using fishing poles and nets, the Ojibwe often use spears to harvest fish, much like their ancestors did.

In the 1600s, when the first Europeans arrived in the Great Lakes area, the Ojibwe had already been living there for at least 200 years. The newcomers weren't interested in the land's wild rice or game. They were interested in valuable minerals like copper, silver, and iron, which were also plentiful on Ojibwe land. The Ojibwe used copper for jewelry and some weapons, but they had never tried to mine it on a large scale.

In 1837 and 1842, the Ojibwe **bands** in Upper Michigan, Wisconsin, and Eastern Minnesota made treaties with the U.S. government. In the agreements, the Ojibwe sold large portions of their land and the mining rights to the government, but they kept the rights to hunt, fish, and gather on it. In return, the United States pledged to make **annual** payments of money, food, and other items to the Ojibwe for 25 years.

The Ojibwe agreed to travel each year to La Pointe, Wisconsin, on an island in Lake Superior (now known as Madeline Island), to receive their payments. For most of the bands, this was a convenient place to gather. It had a long-established trading post and great spiritual significance. It was also home to one of the largest Ojibwe communities in the area.

The Ojibwe leaders were told that as long as they could live peacefully with the increasing number of white people coming to the region, they would be allowed to remain on the **ceded** lands.

In 1850, neighboring Minnesota was still a territory, and Governor Alexander Ramsey had big plans for it. He knew the U.S. government wanted Wisconsin and Michigan for mining. Ramsey decided that if the Ojibwe were permanently removed from their lands and brought to Minnesota, it would leave the Great Lakes area open for the government to use however it liked. And the money the Ojibwe would bring to Minnesota would mean an economic boost for Ramsey's territory.

FACT
The Ojibwe word for La Pointe—Moningwanekaaning—was named after a bird called a northern flicker. It means "at the place of many northern flickers."

La Pointe, Wisconsin, around 1842

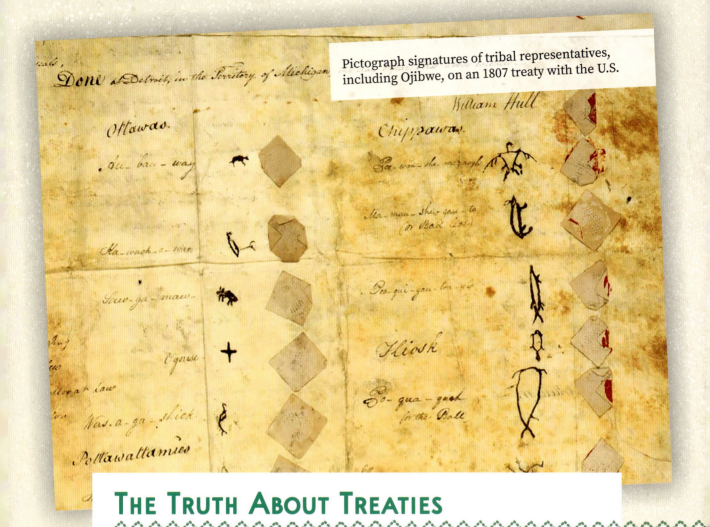

Pictograph signatures of tribal representatives, including Ojibwe, on an 1807 treaty with the U.S.

The Truth About Treaties

A treaty is like a contract. It's an agreement made between governments (in this case, the United States government and a Native American tribe). The treaties often meant that the Native tribes would give up their homelands in return for money and goods.

However, the treaties didn't always ensure a fair exchange. The tribal leaders often had to rely on language interpreters to explain the conditions of the treaties. As a result, they sometimes ended up signing agreements they didn't fully understand. In many cases, the government purposely misled the tribal leaders. And sometimes, the government never intended to honor the treaties at all.

CHAPTER 2

A DEVIOUS SCHEME

"... [We] feel ourselves aggrieved and wronged by the conduct of the U.S. Agent John I. Watrous and his advisors..."
—Chief Gichi-Weshki in a letter to the Commissioner

At first, life was quite peaceful for the Ojibwe after the treaties were signed. They did not suspect that plans were being set in motion that would change their lives forever. In early 1850, Governor Ramsey suggested his idea for the Ojibwe removal to U.S. President Zachary Taylor. Taylor agreed. He issued an **executive order** demanding the removal of the Ojibwe from Wisconsin and Michigan, ignoring the terms of the treaties.

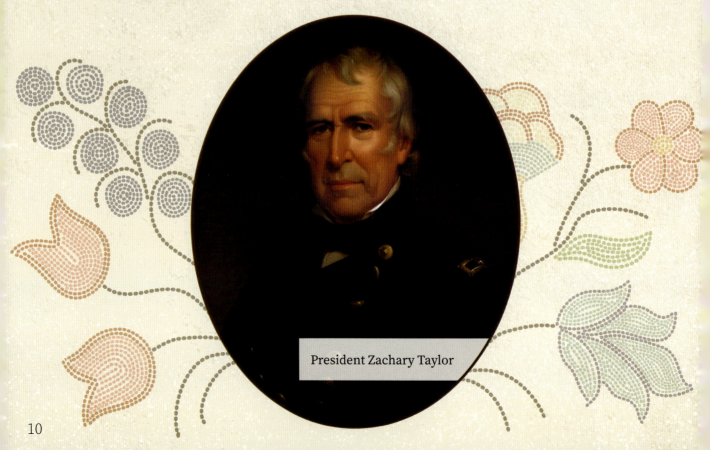

President Zachary Taylor

Alexander Ramsey

When news of the order arrived, the Ojibwe leaders were shocked. They sent messengers to find out if any Ojibwe had broken their promise to **coexist** peacefully with the white settlers, but none had. In fact, most white settlers were also strongly against having the Ojibwe removed. Many even signed **petitions** asking for the removal order to be canceled.

So Ramsey decided to trick the Ojibwe into leaving their land instead. He enlisted the help of John Watrous, a sub-agent at the Indian agency at La Pointe. Together the two men formed a plan to switch the site of the annual payments from La Pointe to a place called Sandy Lake in Minnesota. If the Ojibwe did not make the journey west, they wouldn't receive a cent. The Ojibwe had little choice but to go if they wanted to get the supplies they were counting on for the coming winter.

Ojibwe men posed for a photograph in Duluth, Minnesota, around 1843.

Although the news of the removal order was deeply concerning, the Ojibwe were sure there must have been some mistake. They believed John Watrous when he told them that their stay at Sandy Lake would be short. But Governor Ramsey had other ideas. He knew that if the payments could be delayed for a while after the Ojibwe arrived, winter would set in, and the rivers would freeze over. Frozen rivers would make it impossible for the Ojibwe to canoe home.

Meanwhile, a dispute over whether the territory of California should become a state caused a standstill in the federal government. Many governmental operations ground to a halt—and no one approved that year's payments for the Ojibwe bands. This gave Ramsey exactly what he wanted: an excuse for the delay.

The Ojibwe didn't have any idea of Ramsey's plan to trap them at Sandy Lake. They expected to travel there and back before the first snowfall, with all the money and supplies they would need for the trip. To ensure the removal that Ramsey was seeking, the Ojibwe were required to take their entire families on the journey to receive payment. So that fall, Ojibwe leaders, elders, young men and women, and many children set out from their homes, completely unaware of the scheme that awaited them at Sandy Lake.

What Did Indian Agents Do?

The U.S. government hired white men to work as Indian agents. Their job was to live with Native tribes and act as representatives of the government—distributing payments, keeping the peace between Natives and white settlers, and negotiating treaties. But in many cases, their main purpose was to oversee the removal of Native people away from their lands and onto **reservations**, which opened up more land for white settlers. The agents were also expected to make sure the tribes stayed on those reservations.

Later in the 19th century, the Indian agents gained a new main purpose: encouraging **assimilation** of the tribes. This often meant prohibiting or changing many aspects of Native culture, including their traditions, their language, and in some cases, even their names.

CHAPTER 3

BROKEN PROMISES

"... *the portion for an adult not being sufficient to fill my two hands.*"
—Chief Bagone-giizhig

Sandy Lake, Minnesota, 1850s

In the fall of 1850, about 5,000 Ojibwe people traveled to collect their payments in Sandy Lake. This included the vast majority of the Ojibwe population in Wisconsin and Michigan, and many from Northern Minnesota. For some, the journey was hundreds of miles. Most made the trip by river, in birchbark canoes. They had been ordered to arrive no later than October 25, but it was well into November before the last bands completed the difficult journey. In the end, the date didn't matter.

When the Ojibwe got to Sandy Lake, they did not find the promised money or supplies waiting for them. John Watrous wasn't waiting for them, either. Instead, all they found at the Sandy Lake Indian agency were a lot of broken promises.

At first, the Ojibwe stayed hopeful that Watrous would soon arrive with the payments. After all, they had received their payments at La Pointe for several years without trouble. Surely they hadn't been ordered to travel such a long distance for nothing. Not knowing how long they might have to stay, they set up camp, building bark-covered lodges called wiigiwaams.

But it wasn't typical to have so many families and bands camped so closely together. There was already a small, permanent population of Ojibwe people living near Sandy Lake, which made conditions even more crowded. The Sandy Lake Indian agency's **provisions** and the wild game in the area were not enough to support 5,000 extra people. Food and firewood rapidly became scarce.

Ojibwe wiigiwaams

After a few weeks of waiting, the situation became even worse. The weather grew colder, but the Ojibwe had not prepared to stay at Sandy Lake for so long. Without enough kindling, some were forced to burn their canoes to stay warm, leaving them without transportation to get back home.

Birchbark Canoes

Known to the Ojibwe as wiigwaasi-jiimaan, birchbark canoes were an important part of everyday life for the Ojibwe. They are very fast and lightweight boats, ideal for traveling through lakes and rivers. Birch trees were plentiful in the Great Lakes region, so the Ojibwe could easily find the materials they needed to build and repair the boats. Today, not many people still make or use birchbark canoes, but they continue to be a special part of Ojibwe culture. The artisans who still make them are proud to keep the skills and tradition alive.

Less than a month after the Ojibwe arrived, their food supplies ran out. The agency gave them whatever was available, mostly pork and flour, but there wasn't enough to go around. One Ojibwe leader, Chief Bagone-giizhig (Hole-in-the-Day the Younger), later remembered "the portion for an adult not being sufficient to fill my two hands." Even worse, the provisions were wet, moldy, and too spoiled to eat. Due to extreme hunger, some people ate it anyway and quickly came down with **dysentery**.

The Ojibwe waited for their payments at Sandy Lake for nearly six weeks. During that time, at least 150 died from disease, starvation, and exposure.

> **Fact**
> The measles, a deadly disease before vaccines became available, also ran rampant through the camp due to the poor conditions.

Ojibwe people mourning loved ones at a grave site

CHAPTER 4
THE LONG MARCH

"Tell him I blame him for the children we have lost . . ."
—Chief Eshkibagikoonzhe, about Watrous

The Ojibwe families waited an entire month in bitterly cold temperatures before John Watrous finally arrived at Sandy Lake at the end of November. But they were dismayed to learn he hadn't brought their payments—at least, not all of them. He brought a portion of the supplies the Ojibwe were supposed to receive, but none of the money. Watrous told them they would just have to keep waiting for the rest.

But the Ojibwe had decided they would wait no longer. They were determined to make the return trip to their lands around Lake Superior, even though so many were now ill and weak. In fact, about 200 people were too sick to travel at all. They had to stay behind to be cared for by local Ojibwe.

FACT
The Ojibwe used long, narrow snowshoes to walk across deep snow in the winter.

The route home for many Ojibwe ran along the St. Louis River.

By then, winter had fully set in. Snow was falling, and the rivers were frozen—exactly as Ramsey and Watrous had hoped. Even the birchbark canoes that hadn't been burned were useless on ice, so the Ojibwe had to leave them behind. They were now faced with a much longer, harder trip than before—traveling on foot with their children and elders all the way back to their homelands.

The Ojibwe asked for more provisions for the return trip, but Watrous refused, believing that might force them to stay. Instead, the Ojibwe sold their handmade blankets to traders in exchange for food, which left them without enough blankets to keep warm on the cold trek home. Even so, they refused to stay at Sandy Lake, where they had already lost so many friends and family members. They were determined to get back home.

The Ojibwe asked Watrous to send the rest of their payments to La Pointe as soon as he had them. But Watrous insisted that every person who wanted their share would have to come back to Sandy Lake when the money arrived.

Disappointed and desperate, the Ojibwe began the trip home on December 3. Before departing for his homelands near Leech Lake, Minnesota, Chief Eshkibagikoonzhe (Bird with a Green Bill), also known as Flat Mouth, sent a message to Governor Ramsey about Watrous. "Tell him I blame him for the children we have lost, for the sickness we have suffered, and for the hunger we have endured. The fault rests on his shoulders."

Ojibwe routes to and from Sandy Lake mostly followed waterways.

    The Ojibwe trudged through snow more than a foot deep, carrying their few possessions, their sick children, and the burden of grief and anger that grew heavier with every mile. Despite the bitter temperatures of a Wisconsin winter, they marched across the frozen landscape all the way back to the lands around Lake Superior. Some walked 60 or so miles (97 kilometers) to their homes while others walked more than 200 miles (322 km).

    On the journey home, 250 more people died.

CHAPTER 5

A CHIEF AND A PRESIDENT

"When we left for home, we saw the ground covered with the graves of our children and relatives."
—Chief Gichi-Weshki in a letter to the Commissioner

The failed removal attempt cost 400 Ojibwe their lives—but that was not the end of their problems. Despite the tragedy that had taken place over the winter, Ramsey and Watrous were undeterred. Throughout 1851, they kept up their efforts to have the Ojibwe removed from the Great Lakes region, continuing to insist that they must travel to Sandy Lake to receive their payments. They even threatened to send soldiers to force the Ojibwe to leave their homes again, but the tribes held firm in their refusal.

Several Ojibwe leaders, including Chief Gichi-Weshki, also known as Chief Buffalo, wrote a letter to Luke Lea, Commissioner of Indian Affairs in Washington, D.C. They explained the details of what had happened at Sandy Lake and listed the numerous lies John Watrous had told them. They reminded the Commissioner that they still hadn't received their full payments from 1850. They also asked if they could travel to Washington to state their case in person. The Ojibwe leaders didn't get a reply.

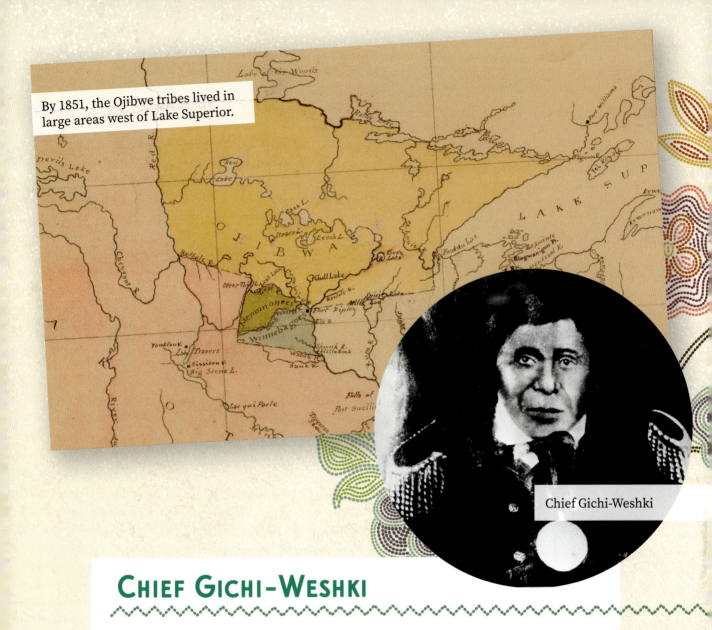

By 1851, the Ojibwe tribes lived in large areas west of Lake Superior.

Chief Gichi-Weshki

CHIEF GICHI-WESHKI

Little is known about the early life of Chief Gichi-Weshki, whose name means Great Renewer. Commonly called Chief Buffalo, he was born around 1759 at La Pointe. He became one of the most influential leaders of the Ojibwe people in the 19th century, helping to negotiate the 1837 and 1842 treaties, and leading his grieving people through the aftermath of the Sandy Lake Tragedy. By that time, he was in his 90s. Though his health was beginning to fail, his determination to seek justice for his people would soon bring about one of their greatest victories.

Time was running out. Chief Gichi-Weshki was concerned that if the government did send soldiers to force a second removal, it could anger his people to the point of an **uprising**, which would almost certainly end in disaster.

At last, in the spring of 1852, Chief Gichi-Weshki knew he had to take matters into his own hands. On April 5, he and five other Ojibwe leaders, along with white interpreter Benjamin Armstrong, set off by birchbark canoe to Washington, D.C. Armstrong later recalled that even 93-year-old Chief Gichi-Weshki helped paddle the canoe at times.

The Ojibwe delegation camping during a storm on their way to Washington

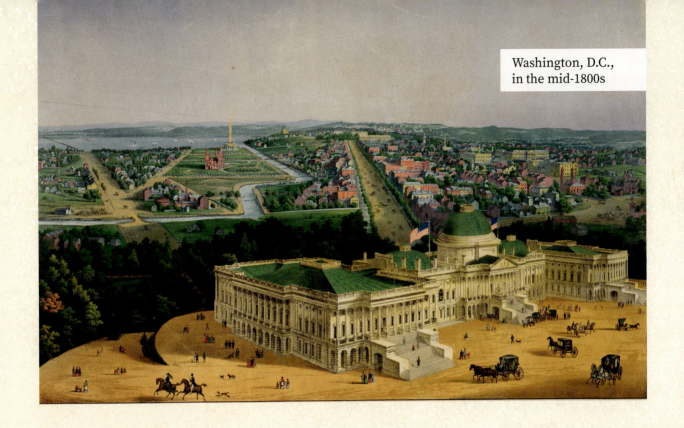

Washington, D.C., in the mid-1800s

They canoed across Lake Superior, stopping in several towns along the way to collect signatures on a petition asking for the removal order to be canceled. When they reached Sault Ste. Marie, Michigan, the Indian agents there tried to make them turn back, but Armstrong insisted that going to Washington was the only way to prevent another tragedy. At last, the Ojibwe were allowed to go on—but they were stopped again in Detroit, Michigan. Again Armstrong argued with the Indian agents until they agreed to let the Ojibwe representatives continue.

Their difficulties didn't end when they reached the U.S. capital. Commissioner Lea refused to help and told the delegation to go back where they came from. Other officials wouldn't go against the Commissioner's decision. It seemed as if the Ojibwes' journey would be for nothing.

Some of the delegation who traveled to Washington, D.C.

But at last, they happened to meet a New York state congressman named George Briggs. He arranged for the Ojibwe delegation to meet with President Millard Fillmore the next day.

When they were brought to see President Fillmore, Chief Gichi-Weshki and the other members of the delegation explained everything that had brought them there: how the treaties had been broken, how the removal order was put in place, and how they had suffered at Sandy Lake. Armstrong presented the petition with all its signatures. President Fillmore listened but didn't give them an answer that day.

Ojibwe members awaiting payments at La Pointe in 1852

The Ojibwe representatives were asked to meet with the President a second time and finally received an answer. President Fillmore promised that he would cancel the removal order and that all future payments would be paid at La Pointe as before.

The delegation returned home in triumph. Not only had they defeated the removal order, but they had done it the way Chief Gichi-Weshki had hoped—peacefully, and without breaking their side of the treaty promises. The Ojibwe people had once again preserved their right to live, fish, and hunt on their homelands, which their descendants continue to do to this day.

Fact

Chief Gichi-Weshki returned to Washington, D.C., in 1855, along with Chief Eshkibagikoonzhe of Leech Lake, to negotiate another treaty. During their visit, an artist created sculptures of them both, which remain on display in the U.S. Capitol Building.

REMEMBERING SANDY LAKE

"May you be strengthened by yesterday's rain . . ." —from an Ojibwe prayer

The Ojibwe have never forgotten the tragedy that unfolded at Sandy Lake. On the last Wednesday of every July, descendants of all the Ojibwe bands who gathered at Sandy Lake return there for a memorial event. They paddle birchbark canoes across the lake, then share a meal and stories of their ancestors. It is a day of mourning for the lives lost but also a day of celebration for the successful resistance of the removal order.

In 2000, a memorial was installed at the site. A plaque on a large stone that looks out over Sandy Lake reads, *Mikwendaagoziwag*. It means, "We remember them."

Ojibwe community preparing canoes for the annual Sandy Lake memorial event

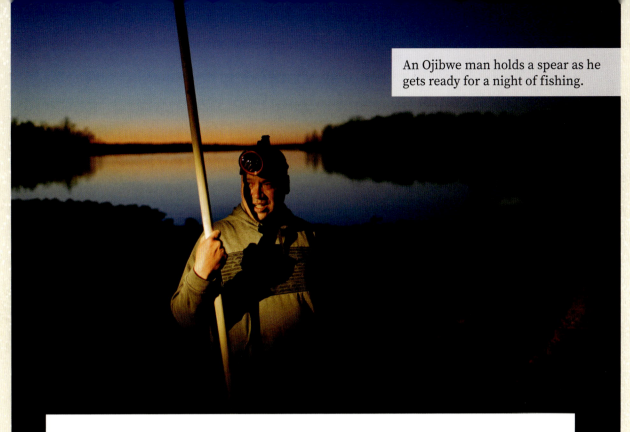

An Ojibwe man holds a spear as he gets ready for a night of fishing.

Author's Note

Unfortunately, the Ojibwe still encounter opposition when it comes to retaining their fishing and hunting rights. In 1974, two Ojibwe tribal members, Fred and Mike Tribble, were arrested for fishing out of season. After a decade-long legal battle, the courts finally ruled that the old treaty agreements *did* allow the Ojibwe to fish outside of fishing seasons and that the Tribbles were exercising their legal rights.

Following that ruling, a series of conflicts known as the Wisconsin Walleye Wars erupted. Protesters gathered at boat landings and tried to prevent the Ojibwe from spearfishing. Despite facing threats, slurs, and several violent incidents, the Ojibwe stood strong and continued fishing. Although these protests mostly ended after the 1980s, Ojibwe spearfishers still report occasional incidents of harassment even now—but they fish on.

TIMELINE OF SANDY LAKE EVENTS

Early 1600s	Great Lakes tribes' first contact with Europeans
1837	The Treaty of 1837 is signed.
1842	The Treaty of 1842 is signed.
Spring 1850	President Zachary Taylor issues removal order.
Fall 1850	Approximately 5,000 Ojibwe travel to Sandy Lake. Around 150 of them die while awaiting payments.
Winter 1850–1851	The remaining Ojibwe return to the Great Lakes area. Another 250 people die along the way, bringing the total loss of life to about 400.
Spring 1852	Chief Gichi-Weshki meets with President Millard Fillmore. Fillmore cancels the removal order.
2000	The Mikwendaagoziwag Memorial is installed.

GLOSSARY

annual (ANN-yoo-uhl)—yearly

assimilation (uh-sim-uh-LAY-shun)—the process of becoming like those around you

band (BAND)—group or tribe

cede (SEED)—to give or yield

coexist (coh-eg-ZIST)—to live together

delegation (del-uh-GAY-shun)—a group chosen for a specific purpose

dysentery (DISS-en-tayr-ee)—a dangerous disease from infection that causes severe diarrhea and dehydration

executive order (eg-ZEK-yoo-tiv OR-der)—an order made by the president

petition (peh-TISH-un)—a request or suggestion signed by people to try to influence change

provisions (pro-VIH-zhuns)—food and supplies

reservation (res-er-VAY-shun)—land set aside by the U.S. government for Indigenous groups to live on

uprising (UP-ryz-ing)—an act of resistance

READ MORE

Sigafus, Kim. *Faye and the Dangerous Journey: An Ojibwe Removal Survival Story*. North Mankato, MN: Capstone, 2025.

Sigafus, Kim. *The Ojibwe: People, Culture, and History*. North Mankato, MN: Capstone, 2026.

Sorell, Traci. *We Are Still Here! Native American Truths Everyone Should Know*. Watertown, MA: Charlesbridge, 2021.

INTERNET SITES

MNOPEDIA: Sandy Lake Tragedy
mnopedia.org/event/sandy-lake-tragedy

Ojibwe.net: Introductions in Anishinaabemowin
ojibwe.net/lessons/words-phrases/introductions/

Wisconsin First Nations: Wisconsin Life, Birchbark Canoe
wisconsinfirstnations.org/wisconsin-life-birchbark-canoe/

INDEX

annual payments, 7–8, 11–13, 14–15, 18, 20, 22, 27
Armstrong, Benjamin, 24–26

Bagone-giizhig, Chief, 14, 17
Briggs, George, 26
Buffalo, Chief. *See* Gichi-Weshki, Chief

canoes, 12, 14, 16, 19, 24–25, 28
children, 13, 18–21, 22

deaths, 4, 17, 20–21, 22, 28

Eshkibagikoonzhe, Chief, 18, 20, 27

Fillmore, Millard, 26–27
fishing, 6–7, 27, 29
food, 6–7, 15, 17, 20

Gichi-Weshki, Chief, 10, 22–24, 26–27

illness, 17, 18, 21
Indian agents, 11, 13, 25

language, 5, 9, 13
Lea, Luke, 22, 25

Michigan, 4, 7–8, 10, 14, 25
Mikwendaagoziwag Memorial, 28
mining, 7–8
Minnesota, 7–8, 12, 14, 20

Ojibwe names, 4

Ramsey, Alexander, 8, 10–13, 19–20, 22

Seven Grandfather Teachings, 5

Taylor, Zachary, 10
treaties, 5, 7, 9, 10, 13, 23, 26–27, 29

Washington, D.C., 22, 24–27
Watrous, John, 10–12, 14–15, 18–20, 22
white settlers, 7–8, 11, 13
wild rice, 5, 6–7
winter conditions, 12–13, 16–17, 18–21
Wisconsin, 7–8, 10, 14, 21, 29
    La Pointe, 8, 11, 15, 20–21, 23, 27

ABOUT THE AUTHOR

Emily Faith Johnson is a member of the Sault Ste. Marie Tribe of Chippewa Indians and grew up on a farm in Northern Wisconsin. She is a graphic designer, writer, and illustrator who loves bringing characters to life through her words and artwork. Emily has always loved history and could often be found reading encyclopedias—for fun—as a child.